4.0/0.5

AB
13⁹⁵

FARM ANIMALS

PIGS

Ann Larkin Hansen
ABDO Publishing Company

visit us at
www.abdopub.com

Published by Abdo Publishing Company 4940 Viking Drive, Edina, Minnesota 55435.
Copyright © 1998 by Abdo Consulting Group, Inc. International copyrights reserved in all countries. No part of this book may be reproduced in any form without written permission from the publisher.

Printed in the United States.

Cover Photo credits: Peter Arnold, Inc.
Interior Photo credits: Peter Arnold, Inc.

Edited by Lori Kinstad Pupeza

Library of Congress Cataloging-in-Publication Data

Hansen, Ann Larkin
    Pigs / Ann Larkin Hansen.
    p. cm. -- (Farm Animals)
    Includes index.
    Summary: An overview of the creature that is more like people than any other farm animal.
    ISBN 1-56239-605-6
    1. Swine--Juvenile literature. [1. Pigs.] I. Title. II. Series: Hansen, Ann Larkin. Farm animals.
    SF395.5.H35   1998
    636.4--dc20   96-299
                                                               CIP
                                                               AC

About the Author
Ann Larkin Hansen has a degree in history from the University of St. Thomas in St. Paul, Minnesota. She currently lives with her husband and three boys on a farm in northern Wisconsin, where they raise beef cattle, chickens, and assorted other animals.

Contents

The All-Purpose Pig

Pigs are funny. They grunt and squeal. They put their feet in their feeders and snort while they eat. They wallow in mud on hot days. They run around like blimps on legs.

Pigs are smart, too. They have been trained to hunt birds and sniff out underground mushrooms. They give us pigskin for footballs, **bristles** for brushes, and delicious ham and bacon. Their **lard** is used to make candles and soap. Old farmers say, "You can use everything on a pig but the squeal."

Opposite page: Pigs are funny little animals.

How Pigs Were Tamed

Nine thousand years ago, people in southeastern Europe began to settle in small villages. The villages had garbage dumps, and wild **boars** came to **root** there for food. The baby boars were easily caught. They were put in pens, and fed every day.

Since pigs like to eat more than anything else in the world, they were happy to stay in their pens.

Today, wild boars and domestic pigs are thought to be different **breeds** of the same animal.

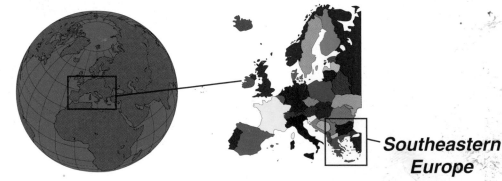

Detail area of Europe

Southeastern Europe

Pigs like to eat more than anything else.

Why Pigs Were Tamed

When people first began to plant gardens in the forests of Europe, it was hard to find enough sunny places. Pigs helped to fix the problem.

Pigs get their food by **rooting**, or digging in the dirt with their noses. This plows up the ground. If there are enough pigs, their rooting will kill trees. This makes way for the pastures and fields needed for farming.

Opposite page: White pigs rooting or digging for food.

How Pigs Are Like People

Pigs are more like people than any other farm animal. Their **digestive system** is very similar to ours. Their hearts and blood vessels are almost the same, too.

Like us, pigs don't like very hot or very cold weather. They can get sunburn and frostbite. They like company, and playing silly games with each other. They are curious, but also lazy.

Opposite page: People watching pigs in a pen.

How Pigs Are Not Like People

Pigs are built for **rooting**. The end of their nose is a hard cartilage disk, controlled by muscles. With this powerful **snout**, a pig can dig through just about anything. Pigs pick food up with their lower lip and flip it back into their mouth.

Pigs are short and very solid. Petting a pig feels like petting a bowling ball. Pigs can't bend to groom or itch themselves, and always appreciate a good scratching from their owners.

A pig has a powerful snout built for digging.

Pigs are short and very solid.

How Pigs Behave

Pigs make a lot of noise. They grunt when they are fed, and squeal if they are surprised. They don't have very good eyesight, but they hear and smell well. Because their hair is so thin and coarse, they like mud on their skin to protect them from bug bites and sunburn.

Pigs like to live with other pigs. In cold weather they will sleep in a pile to stay warm. The most important thing in the world to a pig is food. They push each other out of the way at feeding time.

Opposite page: Piglets pushing each other out of the way to get to the food.

15

Feeding Pigs

Pigs need pretty much the same diets as people. They need the right balance of plant and animal foods, and the same vitamins and minerals. Feed stores sell pig rations that have all these things.

Some farmers mix their own pig feed. A combination of garden waste, table scraps, pasture, and grain will grow a healthy pig.

Pigs also need water in low, small containers that they can't tip over or step in.

Opposite page: Pigs grazing or rooting for food.

Handling Pigs

Pigs are hard to handle. They don't herd well and can dig under most fences. They are too big and stubborn to push around. They will bite. **Boars**, the male pigs, are very dangerous.

Baby pigs can be picked up by their hind legs, but grown pigs must be moved through chutes or lured with food. Pigs that are shown at fairs are trained to move when tapped with a stick on their sides.

Opposite page: Pigs need to be fenced in.

Pig Health

Pigs often get sick. Sometimes they can make humans sick. One of the diseases pigs get is anthrax, which makes a pig weak and maybe even die. There is also **Hog** Cholera, which gives a pig a high fever and loss of appetite. Then there is foot-and-mouth disease, which gives a pig sores on the inside of its mouth. Pigs can also get **swine** flu, which makes it hard for the pig to breathe. This disease can also affect humans.

Opposite page: Like any animal, a pig can get sick if it is not properly cared for.

Baby Pigs

A **sow**, or a mother pig, is ready to have her babies after three months, three weeks, and three days. She gets restless, and makes a nest of carefully chewed bits of straw. Finally, she lays down, and **piglets** begin to pop out! Every 10 or 15 minutes another one arrives–usually 8 or 10 in all.

The sow is too thick to bend around and see her babies, but with her legs she moves them so they can get their first drink of milk.

Opposite page: A large white pig and her piglets.

Growing Up

Piglets weigh about three pounds (1.4 kilograms) at birth. One week later, they are twice as big, and by six weeks, they weigh thirty-five pounds (16 kilograms)! To grow that fast, they have to eat like pigs! Pigs can grow to be 700 pounds (318 kilograms) or more.

Each piglet must get an iron shot at birth if there is no dirt for it to **root** in. If the piglets are in a pen, there must be a **creep**. A creep is a place where the **sow** can't lay on them. A heat lamp is nice in cold weather.

A pile of warm, sleeping piglets is one of the coziest sights on a farm.

Opposite page: Most newborn pigs get their tails clipped.

Glossary

Boar—An adult male swine. All wild swine are called boars.

Breed—Different types of the same animal; like different flavors of ice cream.

Bristles—Coarse, stiff hair.

Creep—A corner of a pig pen where a board or bar about six inches off the ground gives piglets a spot where their mother can't lay on them.

Digestive System—The throat, stomach, intestines and other organs that digest food.

Gilt—Young female pig.

Hog—Full-grown swine.

Lard—The fat from swine.

Piglet—Newborn pig.

Root—Digging for roots, grubs, and other things found under the ground. Swine root with their snouts.

Runt—An undersized piglet. There is usually one in each litter.

Snout—The pig's nose.

Sow—Adult female swine.

Swine—Technically, refers inclusively to all hogs, pigs, etc.

Internet Sites

The Virtual Farm
http://www.manawatu.gen.nz/~tiros/ftour1.htm
A very impressive display including photos and sound. This site is all about dairy farming in New Zealand.

Museums in the Classroom
http://www.museum.state.il.us/mic_home/newton/project/
Prairie Chickens and the prairie in Illinois by Mrs. Vanderhoof's third grade class and Mrs. Volk's fourth grade science classes.

Goats
http://www.ics.uci.edu/~pazzani/4H/Goats.html
This site has photos, graphics, and sound. It has tons of information on raising goats and it even has a goat game.

Virtual Pig Dissection
http://mail.fkchs.sad27.k12.me.us/fkchs/vpig/
Learn how to dissect a pig without hurting a pig. This is a really cool site that gets a lot of traffic.

Sheep
http://www.ics.uci.edu/~pazzani/4H/Sheep.html
This site has everything you would want to know about sheep. Why raising sheep is fun, the sounds sheep make, sheep statistics, basic care, sheep supplies, and much more.

Castalia Llamas
http://www.rockisland.com/~castalia/cllama.html
Chosen as a Hotsite, featured on TV, listed in Popular Science's WebWatch. Full of llama facts, images and stories to amuse and bewilder. This is a cool site, check it out.

These sites are subject to change. Go to your favorite search engine and type in "farm animals" for more sites.

PASS IT ON
Tell Others What You Like About Animals!
To educate readers around the country, pass on interesting tips about animals, maybe a fun story about your animal or pet, and little-known facts about animals. We want to hear from you!
To get posted on ABDO Publishings website, E-mail us at "animals@abdopub.com"

Index

B

baby pigs 20, 24
barns 16
birds 4
bristles 4

D

digestive system 10

E

Europe 6, 8
eyes 14

F

fairs 20
farmers 4, 16, 18
feeders 4
fences 20
food 6, 8, 12, 14,
   18, 20

G

gardens 8

H

hair 14
health 18, 22
hunt 4

L

lard 4

M

mushrooms 4

N

noses 8

P

pens 6, 16
piglets 24, 26
pigskin 4

R

root 6, 8, 12, 16, 26

S

snout 12
sow 24, 26

W

wallow 4
weather 10, 14, 26
wild boars 6